Disney's
HERCULES
THE HERO

DISNEY's
HERCULES
THE HERO

Jan Carr

Illustrated by the Thompson Brothers

DISNEY
PRESS

NEW YORK

In ancient Greece, a strong young god
Hercules! Hercules!

Grew up with folks who thought him odd,
a far cry from a hero.

His strength seemed more than he would need.

Hercules! Hercules!

He rode upon a white-winged steed.
But no one cheered our hero.

With time, the boy proved very brave.
He freed the children from a cave.

He sent the Hydra to its grave
And slew the Cyclops, too.

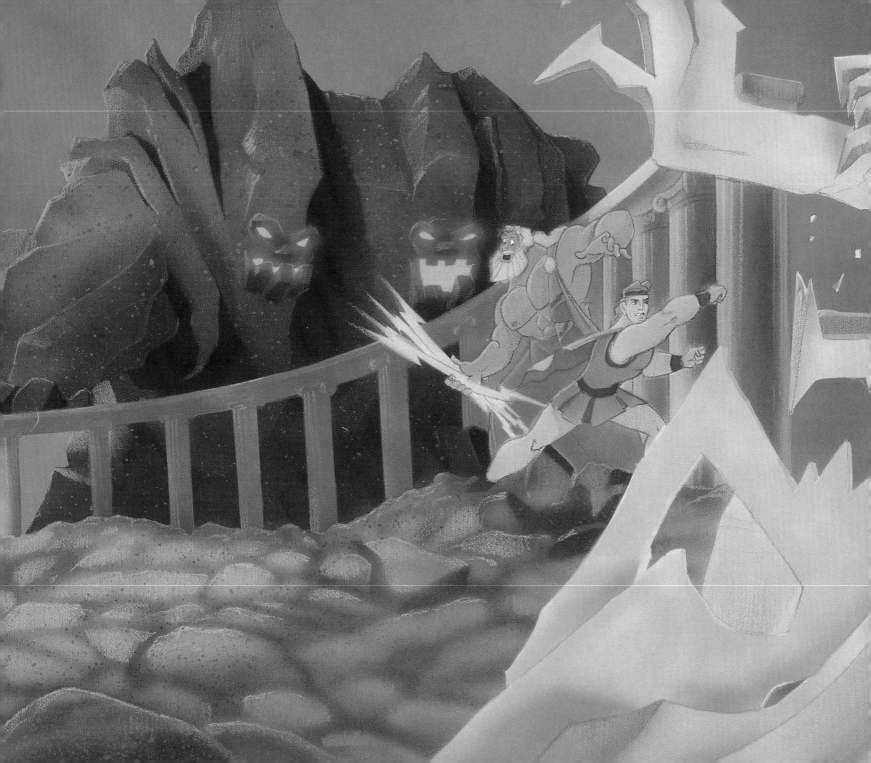

He rescued Zeus. They stopped the war.
He followed Hades to Death's Door.

He saved Megara and what's more,
He proved his heart was true.

At last, this boy who'd come so far
Hercules! Hercules!

Could take his place among the stars.
Hercules the hero!

Pencil layouts by Kory Heinzen

First Edition

1 3 5 7 9 10 8 6 4 2

Library of Congress Catalog Card Number: 96-77806

ISBN: 0-7868-3130-8

WALT DISNEY PICTURES PRESENTS "HERCULES"
MUSIC BY ALAN MENKEN LYRICS BY DAVID ZIPPEL ORIGINAL SCORE BY ALAN MENKEN
SCREENPLAY BY RON CLEMENTS & JOHN MUSKER, BOB SHAW & DON McENERY AND IRENE MECCHI
PRODUCED BY ALICE DEWEY AND JOHN MUSKER & RON CLEMENTS
DIRECTED BY JOHN MUSKER & RON CLEMENTS